Multi-Sensory Together

15 ready-to-use sessions for Bible exploration
in creative small groups

Ian Birkinshaw

MULTI-SENSORY TOGETHER by Ian Birkinshaw
Scripture Union, 207–209 Queensway, Bletchley, MK2 2EB, UK
e-mail: info@scriptureunion.org.uk
www.scriptureunion.org.uk

Scripture Union Australia: Locked Bag 2, Central Coast Business Centre, NSW 2252
www.su.org.au

ISBN 1 84427 164 1

First published in Great Britain by Scripture Union 2005

Scripture quotations taken from the HOLY BIBLE, TODAY'S NEW INTERNATIONAL VERSION, TNIV, © 2001, 2005 by International Bible Society. Used by permission. All rights reserved worldwide. Also from The Message © Eugene H Peterson, 1993, 1994, 1995, 1996, 2000, 2001, 2002, used by permission of NavPress Publishing Group.

British Library Cataloguing-in-Publication data: a catalogue record for this book is available from the British Library.

Cover design by waldonwhitejones of Basildon, Essex, UK
Internal illustrations by Fred Chevalier
Internal page design by Creative Pages: creativepages.co.uk
Printed and bound by Progress Press Co. Ltd, Malta

Scripture Union is an international Christian charity working with churches in more than 130 countries providing resources to bring the good news about Jesus Christ to children, young people and families – and to encourage them to develop spiritually through the Bible and prayer. As well as coordinating a network of volunteers, staff and associates who run holidays, church-based events and school Christian groups, Scripture Union produces a wide range of publications and supports those who use their resources through training programmes.

Contents

Alternative sessions on these same Scripture passages can be found in Multi-Sensory Seasons.

For

Adele, Peter and Sarah

for their unremitting encouragement, patience and love.

Thanks

Thank you to the fabulously creative staff team at St Michael le Belfrey, York. In particular, my thanks to Roger Simpson, a dear brother in Christ, and to Sue Wallace. It was a suggestion from Sue that led to this book being written. I'm grateful to her for introducing us all to fizzy tablets! Thank you to the incandescent Riding Lights Theatre Company and to the St Michael le Belfrey cell group members who have tried and tested so many of these ideas.

And now to him who is able to keep us from falling and to present us before his glorious presence without fault and with great joy – to the only God our Saviour be glory, majesty, power and authority, through Jesus Christ our Lord, before all ages, now and forever more!

Making the most of Multi-Sensory Together

It's a fact – vibrant small groups make for strong disciples and growing churches! Two vital ingredients in sustaining a healthy small group are a balanced 'menu' and committed leadership.

A balanced menu

Have you ever been part of a small group that set out full of enthusiasm and great expectations, and yet before long the life had ebbed away? Some groups get hijacked by the concerns of one or two needy members; some degenerate into worthy but rather dreary Bible study; some groups slide to become cosy social gatherings. Pastoral care, prayer, Bible study, loving relationships – they're all important. But the challenge is to keep them in balance. *Multi-Sensory Together* aims to provide lively and interactive Bible-based sessions that will put Christ at the centre, deepen fellowship and help your group turn faith into action.

The 15 sessions in *Multi-Sensory Together* are built around a common 'menu' approach:

 Getting connected (allow 10–15 minutes)

This ice-breaker will get everyone involved and sharing together from the very beginning. It is easy to see the value of this part of a session when a group is just starting out or when new people have recently joined, but even if you have known each other for a long time you will often be surprised at what you discover.

 Touching God (allow 15–20 minutes)

Jesus encouraged his followers to engage with God through all their senses. For example:

> **Look** at the birds of the air – Matthew 6:26.
> My sheep **listen** to my voice – John 10:27.
> **Touch** me and see – Luke 24:39.
> Take and **eat**; this is my body – Matthew 26:26.
> She has done a beautiful thing (when Mary poured sweet-**smelling** perfume over Jesus) – Mark 14:6.

A small group is the ideal context for exploring multi-sensory worship.

 Living Scripture (allow 40–45 minutes)

The aim is to search the Scriptures, but also to allow the Scriptures to search us. 'All Scripture is God-breathed and is useful for teaching, rebuking, correcting and training in righteousness' (2 Timothy 3:16). Come expecting to be encouraged, challenged, changed.

The **Living Scripture** questions are mainly based on the TNIV (*Today's New International Version*), but try reading the passage from *The Dramatised Bible* sometimes. Different voices will help bring the text to life. Take a few moments to pray that God will inspire your discussion before you consider the questions.

Sometimes **Touching God** comes before **Living Scripture**, and sometimes afterwards as a response.

Reaching out (allow 15–20 minutes)

It is easy to skip over this part of the meeting, particularly if you have let an earlier section run on too long. A group that stops looking outwards will soon become stagnant. **Reaching out** often includes an idea for a social activity as a great way of drawing new people into the group. Plan one into your programme from time to time.

 Digging deeper

Suggestions for further exploration. The bookmarks can be copied and given out to group members to take home.

Leading a group

Some people shy away from leadership because they feel they do not know enough about the Bible, but a good small group leader is more likely to have pastoral gifts than an expert knowledge of Scripture. Here are a few pointers towards effective leadership. For more help, see Mike Law's excellent book *Small Groups Growing Churches*, Scripture Union, 2003.

Prepare well

Each of the sessions in *Multi-Sensory Together* includes optional material. Look ahead and decide which of the suggestions are right for your group. Many of the ideas require some advance preparation. Have everything ready before people arrive so you can concentrate on making them welcome. Don't be afraid to use the ideas as a spring-board for your own ideas. Add your own touches; mix and match activities to suit the particular needs of your group.

Pass it on

Sharing out responsibility for different parts of the meeting will strengthen the group. Work towards a rota where different people lead different sections each time. Meet in various homes so that everyone has the opportunity to practise hospitality (Romans 12:13). Appoint an assistant leader and let them run the meeting from time to time. If the group becomes too big to fit into one home, your assistant can start up a second group.

People-minded

Be people-focused rather than programme-driven. Hospitality is important. Timing is also important – start promptly and don't overrun. If you go on too late, people might think twice about coming back next time. Be aware of the quieter members and draw them in with a simple but direct question sometimes (eg 'Chris, what do you think?'). But be sensitive. If someone does not turn up, get in touch before the next meeting. The aim is not to pressurise people, but to let them know they matter.

Pray

Pray regularly – daily if possible – for the members of your group.

Finally

Finally, many of the ideas in *Multi-Sensory Together* have been used effectively in all sorts of gatherings, large and small. You'll find most can be adapted for school assemblies, retreats, quiet days, camps, conferences, training events, church services, prayer meetings, etc. Step out and experiment. Let your imagination fly!

1 The great escape

Exodus 12:1–32

A session exploring the story of the Passover and making connections between the Passover and the crucifixion

For almost 400 years, the Israelites lived reasonably happily in Egypt. Then a new king came to power and suddenly everything changed (Exodus 1:8–14). The Israelites were victimised and forced to work as slaves. The Lord called Moses to lead them out to freedom, but at first Pharaoh was deaf to his demands. Not even a series of nine dreadful plagues could weaken his resolve. Finally God revealed his tenth and most terrible affliction. At midnight he would strike down every first-born male in Egypt. The Israelite families would escape by offering a substitute. They must slaughter a lamb and paint their door frames with the blood – a sign to the Lord to 'pass over' that house.

The story of the Passover is rich in symbolism. The Israelites were instructed to eat bitter herbs to remind them of their bitter years of bondage (1:14). They were to make bread without yeast – no time to wait for the dough to rise (12:39; 1 Corinthians 5:6,7). They were to celebrate the event for all time as their defining moment when God set them free and made them his own (6:6–8).

The Passover points forward to our own defining moment when Christ, our Passover lamb, was sacrificed for us (1 Corinthians 5:7,8). Jesus took the old symbolism and gave it new meaning at the Last Supper.

 Getting connected

Either

Evacuation!
Q: Have you ever had to evacuate a building at short notice? What happened?

Or

Luxury items
Q: When you travel, what luxury item can you not do without?

Or

Old Testament Pictionary
You will need: two pads of paper; pencils or felt-tip pens.

Divide into two teams. It is better if the teams can be in different rooms, with the leader positioned in between. One person from each team approaches the leader who gives them the name of the first Old Testament character from the list below. They then return and try to communicate the name to their team-mates entirely by drawing. When someone guesses the name correctly, a second member of the team goes back to the leader. The leader gives them the next character from the list, and so on. Set a time limit of 10 minutes. The winning team is the one to identify the most characters in the time.

Noah	Eve	Jonah	Moses	the serpent
Goliath	Daniel	Joseph	Samson	Jacob
David	Joshua	Esau	Abraham	Job
Solomon	Ruth	Isaiah	Nehemiah	Gideon

 ## Living Scripture – Exodus 12:1–32

1 Why does God say, 'This month is to be for you the first month … of your year' (vs 1,2)? In what ways do these events mark a new beginning?

2 Why was the festival called the Passover (vs 12,13)? What instructions does the Lord give to Moses and Aaron about the lamb and the blood (vs 3–11,21–23)? Which details strike you as significant?

3 The instructions for leaving Egypt are combined with instructions for remembering the event in the future (vs 14–20,24–28)? Why was it so important for the Israelites to remember?

4 '… you were redeemed … with the precious blood of Christ, a lamb without blemish or defect' (1 Peter 1:18,19). How does knowing about the Passover help you understand the meaning of Christ's death?

5 'I have eagerly desired to eat this Passover with you before I suffer' (Luke 22:15). How does knowing about the Passover help you understand the meaning of Holy Communion?

 ## Touching God

Either

Seeing red

You will need: a small table; a cross (a simple shape cut from card or paper); red wool or ribbon; background music (optional).

Set a small table in the centre of the group and place the cross on it, either flat or secured upright with a blob of Blu-Tack. You will also need several lengths of red wool or narrow ribbon, each about 20 cm long. Provide one for each member of the group. Scatter these around the cross.

Encourage everyone to make themselves comfortable, then read the following meditation. Don't hurry; take it slowly and pause where appropriate for people to reflect. The script refers to wool, but if you are using ribbon change the words to fit.

> Look at the pieces of wool on the table. Red wool. Let's consider the colour red for a moment. Is it a colour you like? Do you enjoy wearing red clothes; or having red things around your home?
>
> How does red make you feel? Upbeat and full of energy? Or does red disquiet and disturb you…?
>
> Sometimes red is the colour of danger. A red light says, 'Stop!' Red-hot says, 'Don't touch!' 'Red sky in the morning – shepherd's warning.' Perhaps you've had a brush with danger recently…

Red is the colour of sin. Isaiah said our sins are like scarlet; our sins are red as crimson. We're caught 'red-handed'. Perhaps there's some sin you need to confess to God…

Red is the colour of strong emotions. We 'see red' when we're angry.

And red is the colour of conflict. For the Romans, a red flag signalled war and a call to arms. In the British navy, a red flag said, 'No concessions.' The Red Army. 'A red rag to a bull.' Perhaps you're at odds and battling with someone at the moment…?

And, of course, red is the colour of blood. Red blood daubed on the door frames in Egypt… smeared on the posts and lintels as a sign to the Lord to say, 'Stop! Don't touch!' And then there's the Red Sea – the sea which the Lord drove back to make a way from slavery to freedom.

Red is the colour, too, of the blood of Jesus – our own way to freedom.

Think of Jesus… at supper with his friends, pouring out red wine and passing it around. 'This is my blood of the new covenant.'

Think of Jesus, hauled before the high priest… conflict… no concessions… Think of the crowd… baying for his blood… blood that ran over his back as he was torn with whips… blood that ran down his forehead as the crown of cruel thorns was pressed into his flesh… blood where the nails were driven through his hands and feet – for us…

Red blood – to keep us from the sting of death… our sins like scarlet, washed as white as snow… The Lamb of God – our Passover… In Christ all conflict is finally resolved… In the quietness of our hearts, let's thank him now…

And now, let's each take a length of wool and tie it around the wrist of someone else in the group to remind them that Jesus is their Passover. As you tie the knot, pray for them in silence…

As people make their simple bracelets, you may like to play a suitable hymn or song from a CD. You could finish by praying the Lord's Prayer together.

Or

Holy Communion

'They broke bread in their homes and ate together with glad and sincere hearts' (Acts 2:46). Share together in a simple celebration of Communion. Different churches have different practices, so check with your minister first. If your tradition only allows an ordained priest to celebrate Communion, you may be able to use bread and wine which has already been consecrated in a church service.

Reaching out

Either

Fair trading

The Egyptian Pharaoh made the Israelites work under impossible conditions. Many people are still forced to work hard for very little reward. A simple way we can help is to buy fairly traded goods. Make the decision to serve only fairly traded tea and coffee at your group meetings. Decide who will provide this each week.

Or

Slave auction

Organise a 'slave auction' in your church where each member of the group offers time or a skill to the highest bidder. For example, someone could help with shopping or decorating or dog-walking. If you are a talented artist you could paint someone's portrait. If you can play a musical instrument you could offer lessons to a beginner. Donate the money raised to a charity which supports people who live in tough conditions.

 Digging deeper

Give each member of the group a copy of the bookmark on page 61 to take home.

2 Legally binding

Exodus 20:1–17

A session with a focus on the Ten Commandments

After God had rescued the Israelites from Egypt, he set about keeping his promise – 'I will take you as my own people, and I will be your God' (Exodus 6:7). Through Moses he gave the Israelites the Ten Commandments, or the Ten Words. These were not restrictions – the Lord substituting one kind of straitjacket for another – but laws to enable them to enjoy their freedom to the full. Every loving parent knows the importance of clear boundaries for their children – rules to keep them safe and help them make the most of life. The Ten Commandments highlight the special relationship between God and his people, and his concern for every aspect of life.

The covenant follows the pattern of a political treaty. As with legal documents today, two identical copies of a treaty would be prepared, one for each side of the agreement. The Ten Commandments were written on two tablets of stone inscribed by the finger of God (31:18). It is likely that these tablets were identical copies. The Israelites kept both tablets together in the Ark of the Covenant (Deuteronomy 10:1,2) – a sign that God was living among them.

 Getting connected

Either

School rules

Q: Think back to your schooldays. What is the silliest school rule you can remember? Did you ever break it?

Or

Laws or lies?
You will need: copies of page 14.

Divide the group into pairs. Give each pair a copy of **Laws or lies?** Allow five minutes while they discuss the list and decide which of the laws are genuine and which are bogus. When the time is up, come back together and compare your answers. You can then reveal that all ten laws have appeared on the statute books in various American states!

 Touching God

Either

Mount of Revelation
You will need: a quantity of large pebbles or rough stones; background music (optional).

Give everyone four or five rocks. Spend a few moments in quiet as you recall some of the different names for God that occur in Scripture. You could play a piece of gentle instrumental music during your thinking time. Now go around the group and build a 'mountain', taking it in turns to add a rock to the pile. Each time someone adds a stone, they pray a simple prayer – for example: 'Thank you, God, that you are our fortress.' Or 'Praise you, Jesus, for being the Good Shepherd.' Or 'Thank you, Lord, that you are a Father to me.' Continue until you run out of rocks or names!

Or

Alphabet praise

You will need: copies of the alphabet sheet on page 13.

Give everyone a copy of the sheet. Break into pairs or threes and take a few minutes to think of 26 words to describe God, each beginning with a different letter of the alphabet. Gather together and share what you have come up with. Finally, praise God using some of the words.

 ## Living Scripture – Exodus 20:1–17

1. 'I am the Lord your God, who brought you out of Egypt… '(v 2). Why do you think the Ten Commandments begin with this reminder? Read Exodus 19:4–6. How does God promise to reward the Israelites if they obey him? Do these promises also apply to Christians?

2. Verses 3–11 are about our relationship with God. Why does God call himself a jealous God (v 4)? What idols take the place of God in our society? When we are tempted by these things, what steps can we take to 'dethrone' them and put God back at the centre of our lives?

3. Verses 12–17 are about our relationships with others. Why do you think they begin with the commandment to honour your father and your mother (v 12)? According to Jewish law, the four commandments against murder, adultery, stealing and lying (vs 13–16) begin with the most serious and end with the least serious. Do you agree with the order?

4. How important is the final commandment: 'You shall not covet… ' (v 17)? Is a sinful action more serious than a sinful thought? (Read Matthew 5:21,22,27,28.)

 ## Reaching out

Either

Honour your father and mother

If your parents are living and reasonably close by, do something special to please them. Pay them a surprise visit, or arrange to take them out somewhere, or send a gift or letter to let them know you are thinking of them. Alternatively, why not honour an older person whose advice and support have been a blessing to you? Discuss your plans and pray for one another.

Note: It may be that some group members do not enjoy a good relationship with their parents. It may not be appropriate to talk about the issues in the group, but take some time this week to pray about the situation. Now may be a good time to talk with someone whose wisdom you respect.

Or

Invite a guest

Who can you think of who might appreciate an invitation to join your group? Pray for them now, and make the effort to invite them this week.

 ## Digging deeper

Give each member of the group a copy of the bookmark on page 61 to take home.

GOD IS...

Laws or lies?

Which of the following 'Ten Commandments' are genuine local rulings in various US states and which are false?

1   All citizens are required to take a bath once a year.

2   Barbers are prohibited from eating onions between 7 am and 7 pm.

3   It is illegal to slurp your soup.

4   It is illegal to get a fish drunk.

5   Bees are forbidden from flying over the town.

6   Turtle races are banned on Sundays.

7   It is illegal to eat watermelon on Sundays.

8   Using a yo-yo is forbidden on Sundays.

9   Underwear cannot be hung on the washing line in full view on Sundays.

10   If a woman is rescued by firemen on a Sunday, she must be fully dressed.

3 A leaf from God's book

Psalm 1

A session about God's Word giving life

The 150 sacred songs known as the Psalms were written over several centuries. They were probably gathered together into one book in the third century BC. Psalm 1 may have been especially composed as an introduction. It incorporates themes that are to be found in many other psalms, for example the distinction between the righteous and the wicked, and the future God holds in store for people.

These are themes, of course, that resurface throughout the Scriptures. Martin Luther once wrote, 'The book of Psalms could well be called "a little Bible" since it contains, set out in the briefest and most beautiful form, all that is to be found in the whole Bible.'

'The law of the Lord' (v 2) is a translation of the word Torah. It is best understood to mean God's instruction. Faith is not so much about rules and restrictions but about revelation and relationship with the living God.

 ## Getting connected

Either

Favourite trees
Q: Do you have a favourite sort of tree? Why is it special to you?

Or

Tree memory
Q: Is there a particular tree that you remember – perhaps a tree you used to climb as a child? Or a tree on which you carved your initials? Or a memorable Christmas tree? Share your stories.

 ## Touching God

Either

Leaves that do not wither
You will need: four or five simple leaf shapes for each person, about 10 cm long, cut from green paper; green twine or wool, cut into 15 cm lengths; a paper punch; a large twig fixed into a plant pot by surrounding with small stones; background music (optional).

Put your tree in the centre of the group and take a few moments to reflect on the character of God. Write the words that come to mind on your leaf shapes. You may like to play some gentle instrumental music in the background as you do this. Use a paper punch to make a single hole at one end of each leaf and tie your leaves to the branches of the tree.

When everyone has finished, keep silent for two minutes and simply look at what you have made. Let what you see lead you to prayer and praise.

Or

Leaves that do not wither – collage version
You will need: paper leaves as above; a large sheet of paper; glue sticks; background music (optional).

Instead of tying your leaves to a twig, draw the outline of a tree on a large sheet of paper and stick your leaf shapes into place.

 ## Living Scripture – Psalm 1

1 Psalm 1 speaks of two contrasting ways to live. How does the psalmist describe people who ignore God and go their own way (v 1)? What does the psalm convey about their attitudes, their behaviour, their future (vs 4,5)?

2 Reflecting on the law of the Lord is like putting down roots and soaking up the wisdom of God. In what ways is the law of the Lord like streams of water (vs 2,3)?

3 What do you think it means to be 'blessed'? Compare verse 3 with Galatians 5:22,23.

4 'Whatever they do, prospers' (v 3). Sometimes we struggle to make big decisions about such things as family life, relationships, finances, jobs, education, etc. Does this last part of verse 3 help?

5 Read Jeremiah 17:5–8 together. Does this add anything to your understanding of Psalm 1?

6 Look again at the tree you made together. How could you grow to become more like God? Break into pairs or threes and pray for one another.

 ## Reaching out

Either

Musical meal
The book of Psalms is the songbook of the Bible. Plan a social evening when each person is invited to bring a CD with a favourite song. Include some guests who do not usually come to the group. Share a meal together. During the meal have each person say a little about their choice of music before the track is played. It may help to give people a theme – for example love songs on St Valentine's Day, or comic songs on April Fool's Day, or songs on a holiday theme for a summer barbecue.

Or

Pot plant
As a group, arrange to send a pot plant to someone in need of cheering up. Find an appropriate verse from the Psalms to encourage them. Write it on a card and attach it to the plant.

 ## Digging deeper

Give each member of the group a copy of the bookmark on page 61 to take home.

4 Sorry state

Psalm 51

A session about the serious nature of sin and the joy of receiving forgiveness from God

At the height of his fame King David took a stroll along the palace rooftops. From this vantage point he spotted a beautiful woman taking a bath. She was Bathsheba, wife of Uriah the Hittite. Overwhelmed by lust, the king summoned her into his presence, committed adultery with her, and then disposed of poor Uriah by sending him into battle. The story is told in 2 Samuel 11 and 12. It took the courage of the prophet Nathan to confront David and bring him to his senses.

Psalm 51 has traditionally been linked with these events; it is David's song of lament. The psalm includes several words for sin, each with a different shade of meaning:

> *transgression* refers to crossing a boundary set by God
> *iniquity* means wickedness
> *sin* originally had associations with archery and means to fall short of the target

David is guilty of a great catalogue of sins – lust, adultery, deception, murder, abusing his power as king – and yet note how he approaches God with great confidence (v 1).

 Getting connected

Cleaning chores

Q: Which cleaning job do you enjoy the most – washing dishes, doing the laundry, cleaning the bathroom, dusting the living room, cleaning the windows? Which domestic cleaning chore do you really detest?

 Living Scripture – Psalm 51

You will need: a large sheet of paper and a marker pen to tackle the first two questions.

Take a few moments to pray that God will inspire your discussion before you consider the questions.

1   Draw a line down the middle of a large sheet of paper, dividing it into two columns. Go through Psalm 51 together. In the first column list all the different words or phrases for sin. What does

the psalm teach us about sin? How would you explain sin to someone who had never heard the word before?

2 What does David ask God to do about his sin? Go through the psalm again and, in the second column, list all the actions (eg 'have mercy', 'blot out' and so on). What is the significance of hyssop (v 7)? You might want to look also at Leviticus 4:1–7. Of all the words and phrases on your list, which do you find the most heartening?

3 David acknowledges that sin is about what we are, not just what we do. What do you make of verse 5? How can an unborn baby be sinful?

4 David understands that he needs more from God than just a pardon. What else does he pray for (vs 10–14)? How does God create a pure heart in us (v 10)?

5 How does David promise to show his gratitude to God (vs 13–17)? What is so important about 'a broken spirit, a broken and contrite heart'? What encouragement or challenge do you find in these verses?

 Touching God

Either

The Voyage of the Dawn Treader

You will need: a copy of the book *The Voyage of the Dawn Treader* by CS Lewis (one of the Narnia series).

Read the episode from chapter 7 where Aslan arrives to restore Eustace, who has been turned into a dragon. Encourage everyone to make themselves comfortable. Use this first for scene-setting:

> Lucy and Edmund have been drawn once again into the magical land of Narnia, along with their unpleasant cousin Eustace. Eustace is stubborn and selfish, and his 'dragonish' thoughts have somehow turned him into a dragon. Then the great lion Aslan (the Christ-figure in the Narnia stories) arrives on the scene. In this passage, Eustace explains to Edmund what happened next…

Begin reading from where Eustace says: 'I won't tell you how I became a dragon.' Finish where Edmund says: 'And it may be Aslan's country we are sailing to.'

You could let the passage lead you into praise and prayer or use it as an introduction to the following activity.

Or

Washed clean

You will need: a large clear plastic or Pyrex bowl of water (or two or three bowls if the group is large); some Milton sterilising tablets; pencils.

Have the bowl of water in the centre of the group. Give everyone a pencil and a Milton sterilising tablet – the sort used to clean babies' bottles. Other brands will work equally well, but Milton tablets are larger and easier to write on. Make sure the room is well ventilated.

Encourage everyone to take a few minutes in silence to reflect on their own sin. Then invite everyone to write anything particular that comes to mind on the tablet in pencil. There will only be space for a few words (or symbols or initials), but don't forget that you can write on both sides.

When everyone is ready, read Psalm 51:1,2 together, and then invite everyone to drop their tablets into the water. Watch in silence as they fizz away into nothingness.

Finally, read 1 John 1:8,9 and Romans 5:8. Let the verses lead you into praise.

Or

Praise for the cross
Sing a song or hymn of thanksgiving for the cross.

 Reaching out

Cleaning up
As a group, make plans to help with a cleaning task. For example, why not spring-clean the church or wash cars after worship or weed the garden of a disabled or elderly neighbour or clear up litter in a public area?

 Digging deeper

Give each member of the group a copy of the bookmark on page 61 to take home.

5 Portrait of the artist

Psalm 104

A session celebrating God's creativity

Psalm 104 is a dazzling celebration of the work of God in Nature. It follows, more or less, the account of creation in Genesis 1, beginning with light and ending with humanity. The natural world is a source of wonder, not just for its own sake, but for what it reveals about the character of the Creator. The order and the abundance of creation bear God's thumb print, and he is actively involved in caring for all that he has made.

The psalm is poetry, not science. The Lord is portrayed in magnificent picture-language: wrapped in light as with a garment... riding on the wings of the wind (vs 2,3).

Some of the creatures mentioned are puzzling. Some versions mention the coney (v 18) which probably refers to the hyrax, a shy creature about the size of a large rabbit and equipped with feet which are good for climbing. The leviathan (v 26) is harder to identify. The name means 'coiled one' (see also Job 41:1; Psalm 74:14; Isaiah 27:1). It appears to be some sort of great and terrible sea creature – and yet the playful Creator made it to 'frolic' in the ocean!

 Getting connected

Either

Show and tell
You will need: everyone to bring along home-made items – either something they made themselves or a home-made gift they were given.

Invite each member of the group to tell the story behind their object.

Or

DIY disasters
Q: How good are you at DIY? Have you ever had a DIY disaster? Share your stories and sympathise!

 Touching God

Either

Play dough praise
You will need: play dough (recipe on page 21); clean scrap paper; modelling tools; background music (optional).

Read Psalm 104 together. Give everyone a lump of dough and a sheet of scrap paper to work on. Provide a selection of modelling tools (eg old kitchen utensils). Encourage everyone to create a sculpture to represent a part of the psalm. Allow about 10 minutes. You may like to play appropriate music while you work.

Afterwards, gather the models together and take a few moments to enjoy them. Let them lead you into prayer and praise.

Recipe for play dough

You will need: 2 cups plain flour; 1 cup salt; 2 tablespoons oil; 2 tablespoons cream of tartar; 2 cups cold water; food colouring.

Mix all the ingredients in a pan and cook on a low heat until the dough reaches the required consistency. Knead thoroughly and allow to cool.

You can prepare your dough several days in advance if you store it in an airtight container.

Or

Natural selection

You will need: an assortment of natural objects; bowls of water, sand, potting compost.

Have a collection of natural objects in the centre of the group. Try to gather a good variety of items such as rocks, leaves, flowers, fruit, branches, fossils or shells. Invite each person to select one. When everyone has made their choice ask them to reflect in silence on what the object conveys about the character of God. For example:

– sand is a reminder of the way that God supports us through the 'desert' times
– a branch is a reminder that Jesus is the true vine and we are the branches (John 15:1–8).

Allow about five minutes for this. Finally share your thoughts and let them lead you into prayer and praise.

 ### Living Scripture – Psalm 104

You will need: paper; a hat or other container; some individually wrapped sweets or chocolates such as Celebrations or Heroes.

1 What can we learn about the character of God from this psalm? Make a list of words to describe him.

2 What examples does the psalmist give of ways in which God sustains life (vs 10–30)? How do the different life forms – plants, animals, birds, people – depend on one another?

3 How does God invite people to work with him as stewards of creation (vs 14,15,23)?

4 What does the psalm have to say about the natural rhythms that God has incorporated into creation (vs 19–23,27–30)? What might be the consequences of ignoring them?

5 '… if anyone is in Christ, there is a new creation' (2 Corinthians 5:17). Do you find anything in Psalm 104 which relates to Jesus and his work to redeem creation? For example, compare verses 29 and 30 with Romans 8:11; and verse 15 with 1 Corinthians 11:23–26.

6 God created humankind in his own image (Genesis 1:27). What do you think it means to be made in the image of God?

Give everyone two slips of paper, about A6 size. Ask everyone to fold them and write their name on the front of both slips. Collect all the slips into a hat. Invite everyone to take two slips of paper from the hat without letting others see, checking that they have two different names and that they haven't picked their own.

Everyone should open up the paper and write a sentence or two giving thanks for the person named, beginning with the words, 'You reflect the character of God to me because… '

When you have finished, fold the papers again and place them in the centre of the group, each with a sweet on top. Finally, everyone can collect their own and enjoy the sweets while they read what has been written.

 ## Reaching out

Either

Country walk
Organise a country walk or a picnic. Invite guests from outside the group. You may like to pause in a particularly beautiful spot to read Psalm 104 together.

Or

Home-made
Make plans to send a home-made or home-grown gift to someone you would all like to encourage.

 ## Digging deeper

Give each member of the group a copy of the bookmark on page 61 to take home.

6 Plague and promise

Joel 2:12–32

A session about the message of the prophet Joel and the promise of the Holy Spirit

The book of Joel describes a plague of locusts that devastated the land of Judah (Joel 1:2–12). Even in the twenty-first century, despite satellite tracking and modern pesticides, an army of locusts spells disaster. When conditions are right, a female locust can lay her eggs in June and have as many as 18 million living descendants by October. An average swarm will devour 900 square miles of vegetation a day, reducing the land to desert. The roar of their whirring wings and champing jaws is as deafening as a jet engine.

There are no clues in Joel as to when the catastrophe struck, but the prophet interprets the plague as a warning. The people of Judah were looking forward to the day of the Lord when God would come in power to defeat their enemies, but Joel makes it clear that they would also face judgement. He urges them to repent – young and old, male and female (2:12–17). And the warning is followed by a promise – after judgement will come restitution and wonderful blessing: 'I will pour out my Spirit on all people' (v 28).

In the Bible, the day of the Lord can refer to particular occasions in history when God demonstrates his power. Ultimately, though, the great and dreadful day of the Lord (2:31) refers to the time when Christ will come in glory and every human being will be called to account (Luke 21:27,28; 1 Corinthians 1:8).

 Getting connected

Either

Creepy crawlies
Q: Do you like insects? Which insects give you the shivers?

Or

Stir-fly!
Q: Have you ever eaten insects as a delicacy – for example on a foreign holiday?

 Living Scripture – Joel 2:12–32

1   Joel calls the people to repent of their sin (v 12–17). What does Joel mean when he says, '… rend your heart and not your clothing' (v 13)? Who is to be involved in the act of repentance? What does this suggest about the grave situation they face?

2   It is clear from verse 25 that God sent the locusts. Why would a gracious and compassionate God (v 13) cause such devastation? Do you think God still sends disaster on rebellious people?

3   'I will repay you for the years that the swarming locust has eaten' (v 25). How has God brought restoration in your life?

4   'Then, afterwards, I will pour out my spirit' (v 28). On the day of Pentecost, Peter understood

that God was at last fulfilling his promise (Acts 2:16–21). Who is to receive the gift of the Holy Spirit? Have you ever been helped by a prophecy, a dream or a vision?

5 God sends the Holy Spirit, not only for the benefit of Christians, but to equip us to be witnesses in the world before the final 'great and terrible day of the Lord' (v 31; Acts 1:7,8). Have you ever been aware of the Holy Spirit helping you explain your faith to someone?

 Touching God

Either

Voice from heaven

You will need: four recorded sound effects – babbling water or waves, wind, crackling flames, birdsong. Sound effects are available on CD from some of the larger music shops. A good choice would be *Essential Sound Effects* BBC CD 792. Alternatively you could search the Internet for a free download. It would be best to re-record them onto a tape or CD in the right order. Record each effect several times so that it lasts for about two minutes.

Use these sounds representing the Holy Spirit as a focus for your prayers. Take a few moments to relax and get comfortable. Ask everyone to close their eyes. You may also want to encourage people to hold out their hands, palms up, as a sign of being ready to receive.

As you play the first sound, read the first prayer. Speak the words slowly. Encourage the group to go on praying silently for as long as the sound continues. When the next sound begins, read the next passage, and so on.

> **Water** (John 7:37–39)
>
> '… Jesus … said, "Let anyone who is thirsty come to me and drink. Whoever believes in me, as Scripture has said, rivers of living water will flow from within them." By this he meant the Spirit…'
>
> Lord God, you promised to pour out your Spirit on all people. Holy Spirit, we are parched and thirsty for you. Come and water the dry ground of our hearts. Soak us. Drench us. Refresh and revive us. Come, Holy Spirit!
>
> **Wind** (Acts 2:1,2)
>
> 'When the day of Pentecost came, they were all together in one place. Suddenly a sound like the blowing of a violent wind came from heaven and filled the whole house where they were sitting.'
>
> Lord God, the wind of your Spirit blows wherever it pleases. We can't say where it comes from or where it will go. Holy Spirit, we are unbending and set in our ways. Come and disturb us. Compel and empower us. Come, Holy Spirit!
>
> **Fire** (Acts 2:3)
>
> 'They saw what seemed to be tongues of fire that separated and came to rest on each of them.'
>
> Lord God, Jesus came to baptise with the Holy Spirit and with fire. Holy Spirit, our love is cold, our lives impure. As precious metal is purified in the fire, come and refine us. Purify and cleanse us. Come, Holy Spirit!

moment of illumination? Then put your match into the candle flame to light it. When it flares up, tell the rest of your story. You have until the match burns away (about 20 seconds) to say what happened!

Let the stories lead you into praise and thanksgiving.

Or

Group psalm

You will need: a sheet of paper with the words of Psalm 146:1,2 written at the top and verse 10 at the bottom; several slips of paper; glue sticks.

Begin by reading Psalm 146 together. Then take a few minutes in silence while each person makes up a short verse about God's gracious activity in their own life. When everyone has written out their verse on a slip of paper, stick them onto the prepared sheet between the original beginning and ending. Finally, read out your group psalm.

 ## Living Scripture – Mark 10:46–52

You will need: olive oil for anointing (optional).

1 Although Bartimaeus was blind, he was quick to see the truth about Jesus. What did he understand that others failed to see?

2 Look carefully at the way Bartimaeus responds to Jesus. Can you identify five steps that lead to his healing (vs 47,48,50–52)? What lessons can you draw out about praying for healing?

3 At the end of the story, Bartimaeus follows Jesus. When a person becomes a Christian we sometimes say that they have 'seen the light' or that 'their eyes have been opened'. How does the story of Bartimaeus also demonstrate the steps involved in becoming a Christian?

4 Everyone knows that Bartimaeus is blind, so why do you think Jesus asks him 'What do you want me to do for you?' (v 51). Jesus puts the same question to James and John (Mark 10:35–40. How does their reply compare with that of Bartimaeus?

5 What do you want Jesus to do for you? Break into small groups of three or four and pray for one another.

6 Jesus taught the disciples to pray for the sick by anointing them with oil (Mark 6:13). If there is someone in the group who is ill, you might like to do the same. Have a small quantity of olive oil in the bottom of a little dish. As you pray for healing, dip your fingertip into the oil and then draw a cross on the forehead of the person you are praying for. Use these words: *Receive the healing touch of Christ to make you whole in body, mind and spirit.* Or make up a similar prayer of your own.

 ## Reaching out

Either

Praying for healing

Jesus sent the disciples out to heal the sick. Pray that each member of the group will have an opportunity to pray with someone this week. Come next time ready to tell one another what happened.

Or

Get well greeting

Send a card from the group to someone you know who is ill. Try to find one with an uplifting picture.

 Digging deeper

Give each member of the group a copy of the bookmark on page 62 to take home.

11 Fragrant worship

John 12:1–11

A session looking at multi-sensory worship using the account of Mary pouring perfume over Jesus' feet – particularly appropriate for Holy Week

Worship must have been a smelly business in Old Testament times! The Temple was a slaughterhouse where animals were sacrificed and burnt as offerings for sin. The air would have been heavy with the scent of wood smoke and roasting flesh – 'an aroma pleasing to the Lord' (Leviticus 1:9).

John 12:1–8 describes a different and more fragrant act of worship. Once again it is linked with sacrifice – this time the once-for-all sacrifice of Jesus Christ.

This event happened just a week before the crucifixion. Jesus was the guest of honour at the home of his friends Mary, Martha and Lazarus. During the meal, Mary startled the company by breaking open a jar of perfume and pouring it over Jesus' feet. What's more, she let down her hair (an outrageous thing for a woman to do in those days) and used it to wipe his feet dry. John says the perfume was pure nard – fragrant oil imported from India – and very expensive.

Matthew and Mark include the same story in their Gospels, though some of the details are different (Matthew 26:6–13; Mark 14:3–9). Luke also tells of a woman who anointed Jesus' feet (Luke 7:36–50). Luke's account seems to be about a different event. It's possible that Mary had heard of the earlier incident and was imitating it.

 Getting connected

Either

Aromas

Q: What is your favourite smell? What smells do you really detest?

Or

Aroma memory

Q: Some smells remind us of places or events from the past. Is there a smell that always evokes a particular memory for you?

 Living Scripture – John 12:1–11

Take a few moments to pray that God will inspire your discussion before you consider the questions.

1 What do you think the atmosphere would have been like at the party before Mary anointed Jesus? How might the mood have changed after her actions?

2 If you had been among the guests, who would have impressed you the most:

> Martha – for her practical service?
> Mary – for her extravagant devotion?
> Judas – for his desire to help the poor?

3 What words would you use to describe Mary's act of worship? What word did Jesus use (see Mark 14:6)? What lessons can we learn from Mary's example of worship? Have you ever witnessed an act of worship that made a deep impression on you?

4 If you could spend a whole year's wages (or take a year off work) to serve God, what would you do?

5 What do you think the company would have made of Jesus' words in verse 7? What do you make of his comment in verse 8? Read John's account of Jesus' burial which took place just one week after the incident at Bethany (John 19:38–42). What are the similarities between the way these men honoured Jesus and the way Mary and Martha honoured him? What are the differences?

 Touching God

Either

Touching Jesus
You will need: scented hand lotion; background music (optional).

Pass the lotion around the group and encourage everyone to massage some into their hands. Now ask them to sit comfortably with their eyes closed. Allow a few moments as people still themselves, then use the following meditation. You may like to play some gentle instrumental music as a background, but make sure it is long enough to last through the whole meditation – five or six minutes. Read the words slowly, pausing after each paragraph; don't hurry.

> I wonder… do you like to be touched? A deliberate touch from another person is never neutral. Nothing communicates like touch. To touch my body is to touch me. Jesus lived his life touching, and being touched…
>
> The Word became flesh and made his home among us. From the very beginning of his ministry, people pressed themselves towards him – the unwashed, the unlovely, the untouchable. Isaiah wrote, 'Touch no unclean thing.' And yet, touched by compassion, Jesus let himself be touched.
>
> A desolate woman. She's unwell. Unwelcome. She must not touch anything sacred. Twelve years of distress. 'If I can only touch the edge of his cloak, I will be healed…' 'Who touched me?… Take heart, daughter… your faith has healed you.'
>
> A blind man. 'Lord… our friend… his eyes. If only you will touch him, he'll be healed… ' Jesus takes him by the hand… spits on the blind man's eyes… touches him… and he sees. His eyes are opened. He sees everything clearly.
>
> Others bring babies for Jesus to touch. Touching base with the Lord of all creation. He takes the children in his arms, and blesses them.
>
> A woman at the feet of Jesus. The dinner guests are embarrassed. She wipes his feet with

her hair. The heady fragrance fills the room. The waste – it's outrageous!… No… what she has done is a beautiful thing.

The Word became flesh and made his home among us. Jesus lived his life touching, and being touched.

On the night he is betrayed… at supper with his friends. The room is poised… pregnant. The only sound is the soft splash of water in the bowl and the rubbing of a towel. 'Lord… No! You shall never wash my feet…' 'Unless I wash you, you can have no part with me.'

Later that same night… a kiss. 'The one I kiss is the man; arrest him!' Suddenly… rough hands… swords… clubs. 'Are you betraying the Son of Man with a kiss?' Whips! A crown of thorns! Nails driven through the flesh!

The Word became flesh and made his home among us. He was pierced for our transgressions. Crushed for our iniquities. 'My God, why have you abandoned me? Father, into your hands I entrust my spirit.'

Jesus gave his life… touching, and being touched.

His lifeless body is lifted from the cross and wrapped in linen. Placed in a tomb. Three days pass. It's Thomas who speaks out: 'No, I'll not believe! Unless I put my finger where the nails were, I'll not believe… ' 'Peace! Touch me and see; a ghost does not have flesh and bones, as you see I have.'

The Word became flesh and made his home among us.

Reach out and touch me. Stop doubting and believe… Jesus gave us life… touching, and being touched.

Fade out the background music and allow people to emerge from the meditation in their own time. Share any thoughts or insights before you continue. You may like to conclude by praying for one another with the laying-on of hands.

Or

Touching Jesus/alternative
Instead of using hand lotion you could light a scented candle before beginning the meditation.

 Reaching out

Perfumed present
As a group, arrange to send a fragrant bunch of flowers or some scented bubble bath to someone you know who is going through a tough time. Write an appropriate verse from Scripture on a card and include it with the gift.

 Digging deeper

Give each member of the group a copy of the bookmark on page 63 to take home.

12 Family ties

Philemon

A session based on Paul's call to Philemon to forgive his runaway slave, about the church as a family and the need to forgive one another

Philemon was a wealthy Christian living in Colosse and the owner of a slave called Onesimus (a Greek name meaning 'useful'). Onesimus robbed his master and took flight, making his way to Rome where he encountered the apostle Paul and became a Christian. Under Roman law, Onesimus faced a severe flogging or even crucifixion, but Paul writes to Philemon urging him to welcome Onesimus back – no longer as a slave but as a dear brother in Christ. Paul's short personal letter contains an abundance of family language – brother, sister, son.

Philemon's reply has not survived, but it seems the story may well have had a happy ending. Fifty years later, Ignatius of Antioch wrote to the Christians in Ephesus extolling the merits of their bishop. Ignatius makes the same joke as Paul in verse 11 – the bishop is both 'useful' by name and 'useful' by nature. Perhaps the virtuous Bishop of Ephesus was the very same Onesimus who had once been Philemon's runaway slave!

 ## Getting connected

Before the meeting: photocopy the 'Wanted' poster on page 49 and display it in a prominent place – perhaps pinned on the front door so it is the first thing people see as they arrive.

Either

What's in a name?
Do you know what your name means? Use a dictionary of Christian names to look up the name of each person in the group. Does the meaning reflect your character?

Or

Name appeal
Q: Do you like your name? Why – or why not?

 ## Living Scripture – Philemon

1 What impression do you get of Philemon from Paul's letter?

2 How does Paul describe the following people?

    Timothy (v 1)
    Apphia (v 2)
    Philemon (vs 1,7,20)
    Onesimus (vs 10,12,16)

3 In what ways is the church like a family?

4 If you had been Philemon, would Paul's letter have persuaded you to forgive Onesimus and welcome him back? On what terms? Would you have accepted Paul's offer to pay back what Onesimus had stolen?

5   Martin Luther said of this letter, 'Even as Christ did for us with God the Father, thus Paul also does for Onesimus with Philemon.' What does this comparison reveal about God?

6   Read the following verses together: Ephesians 4:32; Colossians 3:13; Matthew 6:14,15. Why is it so difficult, and yet so important, that we forgive those who have hurt us?

 Touching God

Either

Letting go of hurt

You will need: a candle; a bowl of water; floating candles or tealights – enough for one per person; background music (optional).

Have a lighted candle and a large bowl of water in the centre of the group. Give everyone a floating candle (unlit) or a tealight. You may like to play a piece of quiet instrumental music as a background to the prayers. Encourage everyone to become still, then read the following instructions, pausing where appropriate.

> Is there anyone in the church family (or your own family) whom you need to forgive? Let's take five minutes in silence – time for reflection – as we hold the candles…
>
> Forgiving is never easy. Let's ask God to help us release the people who have hurt us…
>
> After a period of silence, read Colossians 3:13 and Matthew 6:14,15.
>
> Let's take it in turns to light our tealights from the candle and carefully float them on the water as a sign that we are willing to let go of the hurt we've carried, and to release the person from their debt. If there's no one you need to forgive personally, join in as an encouragement to others.
>
> When all the candles are floating on the water, conclude by saying the Lord's Prayer.

Or

Letting go of hurt/alternative

You will need: copies of the cheque on the next page; a small table; a cross (a simple shape cut from paper or card); a paper shredder (optional).

Have the table in the centre of the group with the cross on it. Give everyone a copy of the cheque and read the following instructions:

> Is there anyone in the church family (or your own family) whom you need to forgive for something they have said or done to hurt you? Let's take five minutes in silence to reflect.
>
> If someone comes to mind, write their name on the cheque where the signature should go. You may also want to write down the hurt that has been done to you. No one else will ever see it.
>
> Hold the cheque in your hand and ask God to help you let go of the things you have been harbouring in your heart. Forgiving someone is never easy. If there is no one you need to forgive, write a prayer for others in the group.

After a suitable period of silence, read Colossians 3:13 and Matthew 6:14,15. Encourage every-one to feed their cheques into the paper shredder or tear them into small pieces as a sign that they are choosing to cancel the debt. Scatter the fragments around the cross and conclude by saying the Lord's Prayer together.

Note: It may be that some members of the group become emotional about praying in this way. Encourage them to talk and pray the issues through with someone they trust, either by going aside into another room then and there or by arranging to meet together during the coming week.

Or

Song or hymn
Sing a song or hymn that celebrates the Father love of God.

 ## Reaching out

Restoring a relationship
You will need: Post-it notes.

Do you need to restore a relationship with someone you have just forgiven? Or is there an old friend you have simply lost touch with? Could you pay them a visit, send an email, or make a phone call?

Give each member of the group a Post-It note and encourage them to jot down any names that come to mind. Everyone can stick the notes inside their Bibles as a reminder to make contact during the week.

Or

Photo album
Compile a photo album of people you are committed to pray for. Let the pictures help you focus on one or two people each day.

 ## Digging deeper

Give each member of the group a copy of the bookmark on page 63 to take home.

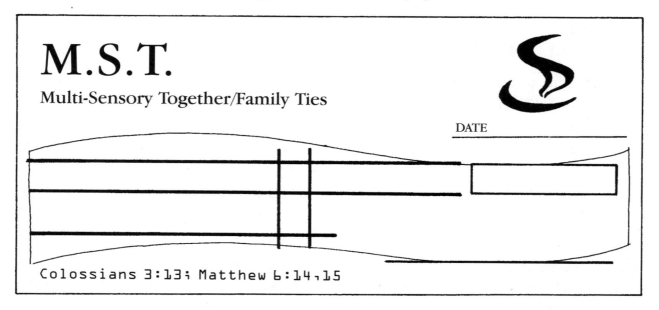

WANTED

Have You Seen This Man?

'USEFUL'

ALSO KNOWN AS 'ONESIMUS'

WANTED FOR THEFT AND RUNNING AWAY.
LAST SEEN HEADING FOR ROME.
ANY INFORMATION, CONTACT:
PHILEMON, COLOSSE

RUNAWAY SLAVI

13 Body beautiful

1 Corinthians 12:12–31

A session about the church being a body

The Corinthian Christians were a tempestuous bunch, torn apart by immorality and infighting. Their acts of worship often dissolved into chaos as members of the church jockeyed for status. Paul confronts their immaturity using one of his favourite pictures for the church: that of the human body. Christ is the head, his body is the church. Just as the various parts of the human body function together for the good of the whole, so members of the Body of Christ with their different gifts and abilities are called by God to work together.

Paul was stationed in Ephesus when he wrote 1 Corinthians, probably in the spring of 55AD (16:8,9). The body of Christ is a theme he would revisit on several occasions in his later epistles (see also Romans 12:4–8; Ephesians 4:4–16; Colossians 1:18; 3:12–15).

 Getting connected

Either

Lending a hand
You will need: string, cut into lengths of about 15 cm, and enough for at least five pieces per person; kitchen timer or piece of music lasting three minutes.

Members of the group should get into pairs, each pair joining hands so that each person has one hand free.

Set a time limit of three minutes using a timer or playing a piece of music. Working together and using their free hands, each pair must pick up two pieces of string and tie them together. Continue to add extra pieces until time is up. Which pair has managed to produce the longest string?

Or

Physically fit
Q: What, if anything, do you do to stay physically fit?

 Touching God

Either

Body language
You will need: a chunky marker pen; a large sheet of paper pre-prepared with a simple outline of a human body in the centre. If you are not confident at drawing find an appropriate picture from a magazine and stick it on the sheet. Surround the image with 'body' phrases such as those shown in the illustration on the next page, leaving space for others to be added.

As a group, spend several minutes thinking of other 'body' phrases and adding them to the sheet. Work together in silence, passing a marker pen around as required.

When the flow of ideas is exhausted, read out Romans 12:4,5. Pause to reflect on the phrases you have written in the light of Paul's words. Share any thoughts or insights.

Finally, re-read the verses and give thanks to God for your church.

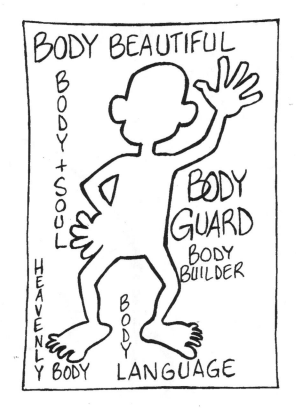

Or

Portraits

You will need: copies of the face on page 52; felt-tip pens; Blu-Tack.

Give every member of the group two copies of the face. Pause to think of some of the people who have encouraged you in the Christian faith; they could be people you have known personally or Christians whose stories have inspired you. Write a name in the rectangle under each face, and then adapt the outline by adding hair etc to make a portrait of the person.

When you have finished, encourage everyone to say something about the people they have drawn. Finally, stick the portraits up around the room so that you are surrounded by the faces. Pray together, thanking God for the people they represent.

Living Scripture – 1 Corinthians 12:12–31

1 Why is Paul's picture of the human body such an effective illustration of the church?

2 According to Paul, how are we incorporated into the one body (v 13)?

3 '… those parts of the body that seem to be weaker are indispensable' (v 22). What does Paul mean by 'weaker'? What special contribution do 'weaker' members make to the church community?

4 '… and the parts that we think are less honourable we treat with special honour' (v 23). When have you been treated with special honour by other members of your church? What effect did it have on you?

5 'If one part suffers, every part suffers with it; if one part is honoured, every part rejoices with it' (v 26). Can you think of times when that has been true for your church?

6 In verses 28–30 Paul identifies some of the gifts given to members of the church by the Holy Spirit. Other people can often identify the gifts we have been given more readily than we can ourselves. Try this fun way of giving thanks to God for one another:

Thumb-thing good
Stand together in a circle. Pause for a moment in silence and think about the person on your left. What gifts do you believe God has given them? What do you appreciate about them?

The first person holds out their hand, with their thumb sticking our sideways, and prays as follows: 'Lord, thumb-thing I appreciate about (name) is… '

The next person (the one who has been prayed for) makes a fist around the protruding thumb, leaving their own thumb sticking out. They pray for the person on their left in the same way. Continue around the group until you have completed the circle with everyone holding the thumb of the person on their right.

 Reaching out

Either

Get physical
Why not plan to take some exercise together? Organise a walk in the country, a visit to the bowling alley, swimming pool or gym. Invite friends from outside the group to join you.

Or

Practical purpose
Do you know someone in need of practical help with a physical task, for example gardening or decorating? Could you offer help as a group? Decide what action you will take.

 Digging deeper

Give each member of the group a copy of the bookmark on page 63 to take home.

14 Living stones

1 Peter 2:4–10

A session about the church being built from living stones

Simon was the most impulsive and inconstant of all the disciples, so when Jesus gave him the nickname Peter – the Rock (Matthew 16:18) – it must have been a great joke among his friends. And yet, as Jesus predicted, Simon Peter did indeed become the rock on which the New Testament church was built.

Perhaps the nickname was in his thoughts as Peter was writing this letter to strengthen persecuted believers, probably in the early sixties AD. He pictures the Christian church as a temple built from living stones, with Christ himself as the most important stone of all. 1 Peter 2:7 looks back to Psalm 118:22 where the capstone originally referred to the nation of Israel. It was Jesus who first took these words and applied them to himself (Matthew 21:42–44).

 ## Getting connected

Inspiring stones
Q: What is the most inspiring building you have ever visited?

 ## Touching God

Either

Character building
You will need: Lego bricks.

Divide into twos or threes and give each group a bag of Lego bricks. Working together, take 10 minutes to build a model that represents something of the character of God.

An obvious example would be a tall structure to illustrate God being our 'strong tower', but try to come up with something more imaginative. When everyone has finished, explain your models.

Pray together, praising God for those aspects of his character that you have called to mind.

Or

Home truths
Move around the home where you are meeting and let the different rooms inspire short prayers of praise and thanksgiving.

For example, you could pray by the front door, 'Thank you, Lord, for your promise that if we knock, the door will be opened.' You might pray in the kitchen, 'Praise you, Jesus, that you are the bread of life.' Or in the bathroom, 'Thank you for washing away our sin.' Choose five or six prayer 'stations'. Let two or three people pray in each place before moving on.

Living Scripture – 1 Peter 2:4–10

1 Peter compares Jesus Christ to four different kinds of stone. What do they tell us about him?

> verse 4: the living Stone
> verse 6: a chosen and precious cornerstone
> verse 7: the capstone
> verse 8: a stumbling block

2 Peter pictures the church as a spiritual house composed of living stones (v 5). He seems to have the Temple of Jerusalem in mind. In what ways is the Christian church (that is, the people) like a building? What does the image suggest about the way Christians are to relate to one another?

3 What is the relationship between Christ, the living Stone, and his people, the living stones? If God is the master builder, what is our part in the process (vs 4,5)?

4 Peter's thoughts flit from the Temple building itself to the activity which goes on inside it. Read 1 Peter 2:5; Romans 12:1,2 and Hebrews 13:15,16. What do you understand by a spiritual sacrifice? What spiritual sacrifices is God calling you to make? Break into smaller groups of two or three people and pray for one another.

 Reaching out

Either

Prayer walk

You will need: a map or plan of the local area (optional).

Take 20 minutes or so to go on a 'prayer walk' of the local area. Break into groups of two or three people and walk the streets together. A map may be useful. Pray for the people who live, work or gather in the buildings. Imagine Jesus to be walking with you and try to see the people and places with his eyes. Come back together at an agreed time and share any insights or observations.

Or

Prayer walk/wet weather alternative

You will need: a map or plan of the local area.

Stay indoors and spread the map out in the centre of the group to prompt your prayers.

 Digging deeper

Give each member of the group a copy of the bookmark on page 63, a copy of the matchbox cover strip on the next page, and a box of matches to take home. Use them to make a miniature Ark of the Covenant.

The Ark of the Covenant was the golden chest that the Israelites carried from place to place. From the time of Moses, the Ark symbolised God's presence with his people. It was the centrepiece of their portable temple, the Tabernacle. You can read the details of how it was made in Exodus 25:10–22.

The Ark contained several souvenirs of the special relationship between God and the Israelites. Most important of all, it was the place where they kept the two stone tablets bearing the Ten Commandments.

1 THESSALONIANS 5:19

MATTHEW 3:11

Don't you know that you yourselves are God's temple and God's Spirit lives in you? 1 CORINTHIANS 3.16

MATCHBOX COVER STRIP

15 Here comes the bride!

Ephesians 5:21–33

A session about the church as the bride and Jesus as our bridegroom; and about renewing our commitment to Christ

Women got a raw deal in the ancient world. A Jewish wife had no legal rights; she was her husband's possession to do with as he chose. Her husband would thank God every morning that he had not been born 'a Gentile, a slave, or a woman'. Deuteronomy 24:1 was interpreted by many to mean that a man might divorce his wife for virtually any reason – even for being grouchy or spoiling his dinner!

In contrast, Paul asserts the equality of women and men under God (Galatians 3:28). He calls Christian men and women to a radical new way of married life characterised by purity and partnership – equal but different. The love of a husband towards his wife must reflect the self-giving love of Jesus Christ for his bride, the church. This is the theme of Ephesians 5:21–33.

The picture of God as a husband to his people begins in the writings of the Old Testament prophets, for example Isaiah 62, Ezekiel 16 and the early chapters of Hosea. The wholehearted celebration of sexual love in the Song of Songs has often been interpreted as a picture of the relationship between God and his people. Jesus took the image and boldly applied it to himself. He identifies himself as the bridegroom in Mark 2:18–20, and the whole theme comes to a glorious finale in the closing chapters of the Bible: 'I saw the Holy City, the new Jerusalem, coming down out of heaven from God, prepared as a bride beautifully dressed for her husband' (Revelation 21:2–5).

Note: if you choose the **Celebration** option in the **Getting connected** section you will need some advance preparation.

 ## Getting connected

Either

Celebration
You will need: photographs or souvenirs.

Ask everyone in advance to bring a photograph or other souvenir of a special celebration they enjoyed. Share your stories.

Or

Wedding laughter
Q: What is the funniest thing you ever saw happen at a wedding?

 ## Living Scripture – Ephesians 5:21–33

1 'Wives, submit to your husbands… as the church submits to Christ' (vs 22–24). The idea of submission to authority is very unfashionable. What does it mean to be subject to Christ?

2 On her wedding day a bride will take great care to prepare herself for her new husband. But

Jesus is the one who makes his bride, the church, beautiful (vs 25–27). What steps does he take?

3 Look at the words Paul uses to describe the church in verses 26 and 27. Which do you find the most encouraging?

4 Paul speaks of the church as the Body of Christ (vs 23,28–31). Are there any fresh insights in these verses?

5 '… a man will leave his father and mother and be united to his wife… but I am talking about Christ and the church' (vs 31,32). What is the hardest thing you have left behind in order to be united to Christ?

6 The passage begins, 'Submit to one another out of reverence for Christ' (v 21). How would you like to grow personally in your submission to Christ and to other Christians? Break into twos or threes and pray for one another.

 ## Touching God

Either

Prayers of re-dedication

You will need: a small table; a white cloth; a cross; petals or confetti; copies of the prayers on the opposite page; cake (optional); sparkling wine or grape juice (optional); background music (optional).

Set a small table with a white cloth in the centre of the group. Have a cross on the table – a simple shape cut from paper or card is fine – and a bowl of petals or wedding confetti.

Give everyone a copy of the prayers. They are adapted from the words of the marriage service. It is important that no one prays them glibly, so take a few minutes to read them through in silence first. You may like to play a piece of quiet instrumental music as you do this. Then pray the words together.

After you have prayed the prayers, write the date and your signature on the bottom of your paper. Keep it in your Bible as a reminder of what you have promised.

Why not conclude with 'wedding' cake and sparkling wine?

Or

Celebration song
Sing a hymn or song which celebrates God's love for his people.

PRAYERS OF RE-DEDICATION

Leader: Hear what Jesus says to us, his church:
I, Jesus Christ, take you, the church, to be my bride:
to have and to hold,
to love and to cherish.
With my broken body I have honoured you.
All that I am I gave for you.
All that I have I share with you.
I will love you, comfort you,
honour and protect you,
today and for all eternity.

All: **We, your church,**
take you, Jesus Christ, to be our husband,
for richer, for poorer,
in sickness and in health,
to love, cherish and obey.
As your body, we honour you.
All that we are, we give back to you.
Forsaking all others, we'll be faithful to you.
In the presence of God, we make this vow.

In silence, each member of the group takes a handful of petals or confetti and sprinkles it around the cross as a sign of their love and commitment to Christ. When everyone has done so, the leader continues:

Leader: Those whom God has joined together…
All: **let no one put asunder.**
Leader: Blessed are you, heavenly Father.
All: **You give joy to bridegroom and bride.**
Leader: Blessed are you, Lord Jesus Christ.
All: **You bring life to the world.**
Leader: Blessed are you, Holy Spirit of God.
All: **You bind us together in love.**
Blessed are you, Father, Son and Holy Spirit,
now and for ever. Amen.

Signed:

Date:

Reaching out

Either

Rejoicing with those who rejoice
Send a card from the group to someone you know who has something to celebrate.

Or

Romantic movie
Arrange a trip to the cinema to see the latest romantic film. Invite guests from outside the group to join you. Afterwards go on to a café or pub where you can enjoy a drink together and chat about the movie.

 Digging deeper

Give each member of the group a copy of the bookmark on page 63 to take home.

The great escape

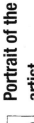

Read the account of Moses' life in the early chapters of Exodus. Ask yourself these questions:

What do you notice about the way God prepared Moses to be a leader?

How did the Lord respond to Moses' doubts?

Looking back on your own life, can you see ways in which God has been coaching you?

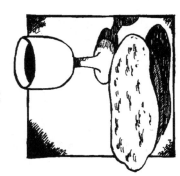

Day 1: **Exodus 1:22 – 2:10**
Day 2: **Exodus 2:11–25**
Day 3: **Exodus 3**
Day 4: **Exodus 4:1–18**
Day 5: **Exodus 5:22 – 6:12**

Then read the story of the Israelites' escape from Egypt.

Day 6: **Exodus 14:5 – 15:21**

The song of praise in chapter 15 is probably the oldest poem in the Bible. Why not have a go at making up a short praise-poem of your own? Base it on your reflections this week. Begin with the same opening words as the Israelites:

'I will sing to the LORD,
for he is highly exalted…'

Legally binding

This spiritual exercise is based on a traditional way of praying known as the Examen of Conscience. It was developed by Ignatius of Loyola in the sixteenth century.

Set aside 15 or 20 minutes at the end of the day. First, be still and remember that God is with you. You may like to light a candle to remind you of Jesus' promise: 'I am the light of the world. Whoever follows me will never walk in darkness, but will have the light of life' (John 8:12).

Read through the Ten Commandments (Exodus 20:1–17).

Now think over the events of the day. Try to recall your feelings.

When were you aware of God's love, or the love of other people during the day? Thank God for those moments, for those people…

What opportunities were there for you to share love with others today? What happened?

Did you break any of the Ten Commandments today? Ask God to forgive you, and to help you do better tomorrow. Look forward with hope.

A leaf from God's book

Set aside time to meditate this week. Find a place out-of-doors or by a window where you can sit quietly in sight of a tree. Alternatively, find a picture of a tree. Make yourself comfortable. Don't rush. Allow yourself time to become still. Read the passage over several times and feed on the words.

Day 1: **Galatians 5:22,23**
Day 2: **Luke 6:43,44**
Day 3: **John 15:5**
Day 4: **Luke 13:18,19**
Day 5: **Revelation 2:7**
Day 6: **Revelation 22:1,2**

Sorry state

Read Psalm 51 and pick out your favourite verses. Write them on Post-it notes and attach them to your bathroom mirror. Each time you wash this week, read the verses and thank God for his mercy.

Here are some other verses you might like to display in the bathroom!

Jesus said, 'Unless I wash you, you have no part with me' (John 13:8).

'Come near to God and he will come near to you. Wash your hands, you sinners, and purify your hearts, you double-minded' (James 4:8).

Portrait of the artist

Over the next six days, read and reflect on the account of creation in Genesis 1. Don't hurry – ask the Holy Spirit to help you appreciate something new about the character of God each day.

If you are able to pray each day in the same place, you may like to gather a collection of objects or pictures as a focus for your prayers. Add a new item to the collection each day. Here are some suggestions:

Day 1: **Genesis 1:1–5**
candle
Day 2: **Genesis 1:6–8**
bowl of water
Day 3: **Genesis 1:9–13**
piece of fruit
Day 4: **Genesis 1:14–19**
clock
Day 5: **Genesis 1:20–23**
feather
Day 6: **Genesis 1:24–31**
family photograph

Plague and promise

'Return to me with all your heart, with fasting....' (Joel 2:12). Set aside a day this week for prayer and fasting. Try missing out two meals, perhaps breakfast and lunch. If possible, agree to fast on the same day as others in the group, so that you can support one another in prayer.

Why fast?

Fasting is worship.

Jesus encouraged his followers to fast. 'When you fast...' (Matthew 6:16).

Jesus promised that God will bless those who fast (Matthew 6:17,18).

Fasting helps us 'tune in' to God (eg Acts 13:2,3).

When you fast...

Set aside special times for prayer.

Let your fast be a secret between you and God (Matthew 6:16–18).

Healthy fasting

Do not fast if you have any anxieties about your health.

Drink plenty of water.

When you end your fast, eat a little less than usual.

Whale of a tale

Re-reading the story of Jonah, design a coat of arms for him. Think about:

What symbols would you include to represent his character?

How does the Lord deal with Jonah?

Choose a verse from the story to be Jonah's motto.

How does Jonah remind you of yourself?

What do you need to say to God?

What is God saying to you through the story?

Or

Get hold of a copy of *Moby Dick* by Herman Melville.

Chapter 9 is a sermon on the story of Jonah: *Shipmates, this book...is one of the smallest strands in the mighty cable of the Scriptures. Yet what depths of the soul does Jonah's deep sealine sound!*

Read the chapter. What do you find in it to inspire or challenge you?

Wise guys

Make a map of your own faith journey this week, with a line to represent the twists and turns your life has taken.

What were the 'mountain-top' moments of epiphany when you came to understand more about God?

When have you been through 'desert' experiences, when you have felt spiritually dry?

Have there been times when you felt confused and 'couldn't see the wood for the trees'?

Who were your guides along the way?

Represent them all on the map. Take a little time each day to add to your map, praying as you do so.

What does God want to show you about the journey you have made?

Gone fishing

Jesus demonstrated his power over nature on several occasions. As you read each passage, look for the following:

  an encouragement

  a challenge

  a question

  a prayer

  a verse or phrase to carry through the day

Day 1: **Luke 8:22–25**
calming a storm

Day 2: **John 6:5–14**
feeding 5000 people

Day 3: **Matthew 14:22–33**
walking on water

Day 4: **Mark 8:1–10**
feeding 4000 people

Day 5: **Matthew 17:24–27**
the coin and the fish

Day 6: **John 2:1–11**
water becomes wine

Seeing is believing

Here are six stories about people who were healed by Jesus. As you read them each day, ask these questions:

What is the problem?

What does Jesus do/say?

How does the person respond?

What can we learn about praying for those who are ill?

Day 1: **Mark 1:40–45**
a man with leprosy

Day 2: **Mark 2:1–12**
a paralysed man

Day 3: **Mark 5:25–34**
a sick woman

Day 4: **Mark 5:21–24,35–43**
a dead girl

Day 5: **Mark 7:24–30**
a woman with faith

Day 6: **Mark 8:22–26**
a blind man

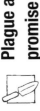

Fragrant worship

Jesus encouraged his followers to worship through their God-given senses. Take time this week to worship through the senses. Here are three suggestions:

1 Read **Matthew 6:26–30**. Go out for a walk in the country or your local park – not a strenuous hike but a gentle stroll. Slow your pace right down and take time to be aware of your surroundings and their impact on your senses. What do you see?. What do you smell? What do you hear? Pause to take in the delicate arrangement of petals on a wild flower, or to feel the texture of stones in a wall. Let the experience stir you to praise God.

2 Choose a natural object – for example a plant, a rock or a piece of driftwood, and make a drawing of it. The quality of your artwork doesn't matter (especially as you don't have to show it to anyone). The important thing is that you look closely and let it lead you into an appreciation of God's creativity.

3 Eat a bar of chocolate or a delicious piece of fruit or some other food you especially enjoy. Eat it slowly and savour the feel and flavour of each bite. 'Taste and see that the LORD is good' (Psalm 34:8)! With each mouthful, thank God for some particular person or blessing.

Family ties

Joseph is his father's favourite. His envious brothers sell him into slavery, expecting never to see him again. They trick their father into believing he is dead. But God is with Joseph. He becomes prime minister of Egypt and his foresight means the country prospers during a period of famine. His brothers come begging for food. It is 22 years since they last met but he recognises them instantly. Instead of condemning them, Joseph forgives…

What do these passages have to say about family ties and forgiveness?

Day 1: **Genesis 37**

Day 2: **Genesis 45**

Day 3: **Luke 15:11–24**

Day 4: **Luke 15:25–32**

Day 5: **Matthew 18:21–27**

Day 6: **Matthew 18:28–35**

Body beautiful

'Now you are the body of Christ, and each one of you is a part of it … And now I will show you the most excellent way' (1 Corinthians 12:27,31).

Paul continues his teaching on the body of Christ with his famous chapter about love.

Fill in the blanks below, substituting your own name for the word 'love'.

1 Corinthians 13:4–7

_____ is patient, _____ is kind. _____ does not envy, _____ does not boast, _____ is not proud. _____ does not dishonour others, _____ is not self-seeking, _____ is not easily angered, _____ keeps no record of wrongs. _____ does not delight in evil but rejoices with the truth. _____ always protects, _____ always trusts, _____ always hopes, _____ always perseveres.

Now read the whole passage back to yourself, aloud if possible. Spend some time reflecting on how it feels. Pray, asking God to help you become better at loving others.

You may want to focus your prayers on a different phrase of the passage each day this week.

Living stones

Turn a matchbox into your own miniature Ark of the Covenant! Cut out the cover strip provided and glue it around a matchbox so the picture of the original Ark is on top.

Fire is a symbol of the Holy Spirit, so carry the matchbox with you this week as a reminder that the Holy Spirit lives in you. Or you could empty out the matches and place some other small souvenir of your personal journey with God inside. Each time you rediscover the Ark in your pocket or handbag call to mind God's presence with you and pray silently for the people you are with or the situation you are in.

Meditate on these verses:

1 Thessalonians 5:19

Matthew 3:11

1 Corinthians 3:16

Here comes the bride!

Take time to read the passage and reflect on the question. Let your thoughts lead you into prayer.

Day 1: **Song of Songs 2**

This poem celebrates the love between a man and a woman. Do you see any parallels with the love between Christ and his church?

Day 2: **John 3:22–30**

In what ways is John the Baptist like a 'best man'?

Day 3: **Matthew 25:1–13**

What do you think the oil represents in this parable?

Day 4: **Hosea 2:14–20**

Hosea's wife was unfaithful, but Hosea loved her and brought her home. Their marriage becomes a picture of God's love for his people. How faithful to Christ is the church in our generation?

Day 5: **John 2:1–11**

'Fill the water pots with water, fill them to the very brim;

He will honour all your trusting – leave the miracle to him.'

What aspect of your life would you most like Jesus to transform?

Day 6: **Revelation 19:5–9; 21:2–5**

'Fine linen, bright and clean, was given her to wear' (19:8).

Meditate on this verse. You may like to carry a piece of white fabric in your pocket to remind you of it through the day.

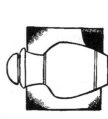

Other books in the Multi-Sensory series

✳ fresh ✳ innovative ✳ imaginative ✳ inspirational ✳ practical

MULTI-SENSORY CHURCH

Over 30 ready-to-use ideas for creative churches and small groups

Sue Wallace

This invaluable resource includes a variety of ways of exploring the senses to expand your understanding and grow your delight in prayer, liturgy, Bible reading, celebration, labyrinths and much more.

MULTI-SENSORY PRAYER

Over 60 ready-to-use ideas for creative churches and small groups

Sue Wallace

Ways to use the senses to enrich your prayer experience – using everything from candles and broken pottery to nuts, leaves, newspapers, dough and mirrors!

MULTI-SENSORY SCRIPTURE

50 innovative ideas for exploring the Bible in churches and small groups

Sue Wallace

Bible-focused ideas to expand understanding and grow delight in many aspects of confession, intercession, meditation and much more.

MULTI-SENSORY SEASONS

15 ready-to-use Bible-based sessions through the seasons for creative small groups

Wendy Rayner and Annie Slade

Complete small group sessions based on a range of Biblical material from both Old and New Testaments that can be used any time or tied to a specific season of the church calendar.

––––––––

This series is just part of a wide range of resources for churches and small groups published by Scripture Union. There's also a free online magazine about the world of small groups called church@home. Go to **www.scriptureunion.org.uk/churchathome**

SU publications are available from Christian bookshops, on the Internet or via mail order. You can:

phone SU's mail order line: 0845 0706006

email info@scriptureunion.org.uk

fax 01908 856020

log on to www.scriptureunion.org.uk

write to SU Mail Order, PO Box 5148, Milton Keynes MLO, MK2 2YX